GILA MONSTERS

by Imogen Kingsley

AMICUS | AMICUS INK

Amicus High Interest and Amicus Ink are published by Amicus
P.O. Box 1329, Mankato, MN 56002
www.amicuspublishing.us

Library of Congress Cataloging-in-Publication Data
Names: Kingsley, Imogen, author.
Title: Gila monsters / by Imogen Kingsley.
Description: Mankato, Minnesota : Amicus/Amicus Ink, [2019] | Series:
Lizards in the wild | Audience: K to Grade 3. | Includes index.
Identifiers: LCCN 2018004179| ISBN 9781681515571 (library binding) |
ISBN 9781681523958 (paperback) | ISBN 9781681515953 (ebook)
Subjects: LCSH: Gila monster--Juvenile literature.
Classification: LCC QL666.L247 K56 2019 | DDC 597.95/952--dc23
LC record available at https://lccn.loc.gov/2018004179

Photo Credits: Shutterstock/fivespots, cover, 2, 22, Kris Wiktor, 5; Alamy/
Jared Hobbs, 6-7, Rick & Nora Bowers, 9, 14, 18, Norma Jean Gargasz, 10;
Getty/Danita Delimont, 13, Tim Flach, 17; AnimalsAnimals/Paul Freed,
20-21

Editor: Mary Ellen Klukow
Designer: Peggie Carley
Photo Researcher: Holly Young

Printed in China

HC 10 9 8 7 6 5 4 3 2 1
PB 10 9 8 7 6 5 4 3 2 1

TABLE OF CONTENTS

A DESERT LIZARD

A Gila monster sticks out his head. His black eyes look. His tongue flicks and smells the air. It is time to hunt!

BIG AND BEADED

The Gila monster is big! It can be 2 feet (0.6 m) long. That is why it is called a "dragon." It has black and orange scales. They look like beads. Their bright color warns **predators** to stay away!

KEEPING WARM

Gila monsters live in the Southwest. They like desert and **scrubland**. It is hot and dry there. Gilas are cold-blooded. They need the sun to keep warm.

COOL AND SAFE

A Gila can get too hot in the sun.

But it is a good digger. It has

strong legs and sharp claws. It

digs a **burrow**. It is cool there.

Check This Out

A Gila spends most of its life in its burrow.

A SLOW MOVER

A Gila monster moves slowly. It is not worried about being chased. It has very few predators. Its bright spots warn animals not to attack.

WATCH OUT

A Gila monster bites if it is attacked. **Venom** flows from its teeth into the attacker. This teaches predators to stay away. It also uses venom on its **prey.**

Check This Out
A bite from a Gila monster would not kill you. But it would hurt!

ON THE HUNT

A Gila is on the hunt. She finds a quail's nest. She can eat a nest in seconds. She also hunts mice and rabbits.

Check This Out
A Gila can swallow small eggs whole.

A THICK TAIL

A Gila monster does not eat often.
It might only eat five times a year!
It stores fat in its tail. The Gila
won't starve if it has extra fat.

YOUNG GILAS

Gilas mate in spring. Then the female lays eggs. The eggs hatch in the winter. The **hatchlings** leave the nest in spring. They are ready to explore their world!

21

A LOOK AT A GILA MONSTER

thick tail

flat head

bead-like scales

sharp claws

forked tongue

WORDS TO KNOW

burrow An animal home that is underground.

hatchling A young Gila monster.

predator An animal that hunts other animals for food.

prey An animal hunted by other animals for food.

scrubland A dry habitat that has a few woody shrubs.

venom Poison from an animal.

LEARN MORE

Books

Black, Vanessa. *Gila Monsters*. Minneapolis: Jump!, 2016.

Brett, Flora. *Get to Know Gila Monsters*. North Mankato, Minn.: Capstone, 2015.

Phillips, Dee. *Gila Monster's Burrow*. New York: Bearport Publishing, 2015.

Websites

DK Find Out!: Lizards
https://www.dkfindout.com/us/animals-and-nature/reptiles/lizards/

National Geographic Kids: The Gila Monster
https://kids.nationalgeographic.com/animals/gila-monster/

The Desert Museum: The Gila Monster
https://www.desertmuseum.org/kids/oz/long-fact-sheets/Gila%20Monster.php

INDEX